ANIMALS OF THE...

Fennec Foxes

by Patrick Perish

BLASTOFF! READERS 2

BELLWETHER MEDIA • MINNEAPOLIS, MN

Note to Librarians, Teachers, and Parents:

Blastoff! Readers are carefully developed by literacy experts and combine standards-based content with developmentally appropriate text.

Level 1 provides the most support through repetition of high-frequency words, light text, predictable sentence patterns, and strong visual support.

Level 2 offers early readers a bit more challenge through varied simple sentences, increased text load, and less repetition of high-frequency words.

Level 3 advances early-fluent readers toward fluency through increased text and concept load, less reliance on visuals, longer sentences, and more literary language.

Level 4 builds reading stamina by providing more text per page, increased use of punctuation, greater variation in sentence patterns, and increasingly challenging vocabulary.

Level 5 encourages children to move from "learning to read" to "reading to learn" by providing even more text, varied writing styles, and less familiar topics.

Whichever book is right for your reader, Blastoff! Readers are the perfect books to build confidence and encourage a love of reading that will last a lifetime!

This edition first published in 2019 by Bellwether Media, Inc.

No part of this publication may be reproduced in whole or in part without written permission of the publisher. For information regarding permission, write to Bellwether Media, Inc., Attention: Permissions Department, 6012 Blue Circle Drive, Minnetonka, MN 55343.

Library of Congress Cataloging-in-Publication Data

Names: Perish, Patrick, author.
Title: Fennec Foxes / by Patrick Perish.
Description: Minneapolis, MN : Bellwether Media, Inc., 2019. | Series: Blastoff! Readers. Animals of the Desert | Audience: Age 5-8. | Audience: K to Grade 3. | Includes bibliographical references and index.
Identifiers: LCCN 2018030985 (print) | LCCN 2018037373 (ebook) | ISBN 9781618916334 (ebook) | ISBN 9781626179226 (hardcover : alk. paper)
Subjects: LCSH: Fennec--Juvenile literature. | Desert animals--Juvenile literature.
Classification: LCC QL737.C22 (ebook) | LCC QL737.C22 P436 2019 (print) | DDC 599.776--dc23
LC record available at https://lccn.loc.gov/2018030985

Text copyright © 2019 by Bellwether Media, Inc. BLASTOFF! READERS and associated logos are trademarks and/or registered trademarks of Bellwether Media, Inc. SCHOLASTIC, CHILDREN'S PRESS, and associated logos are trademarks and/or registered trademarks of Scholastic Inc., 557 Broadway, New York, NY 10012.

Editor: Rebecca Sabelko   Designer: Josh Brink

Printed in the United States of America, North Mankato, MN

Table of Contents

Life in the Desert	4
Escaping the Heat	10
On the Hunt	16
Glossary	22
To Learn More	23
Index	24

Life in the Desert

Fennec foxes are made to survive in the deserts of northern Africa.

This dry **biome** has bushes, grasses, and sandy **dunes**.

Fennec Fox Range

range =

Deserts get very hot during the day. But they get cold at night.

Fennec foxes have **adapted** to the hot and the cold!

Big ears keep fennec foxes cool by letting out heat.

Their thick **coats** keep the foxes warm on chilly nights.

Special Adaptations

large ears

thick coat

furry feet

Escaping the Heat

Fennec foxes' fur **reflects** the hot sun. It keeps the foxes from getting too hot.

Their sandy color helps them hide from **predators**.

Furry feet keep fennec foxes from getting burned by hot sand.

Their feet also help them climb dunes covered in loose sand.

sand dunes

13

Fennec foxes are **nocturnal**. They rest during the day.

Their **burrows** stay cool and protect them from predators.

burrow

On the Hunt

Fennec foxes' big ears help them hear **rodents** moving under the sand.

Their quick paws dig the **prey** out. Then, they **pounce**!

Food can be hard to find in the desert. Fennec foxes cannot be picky!

These **omnivores** snack on rodents, birds, **insects**, plants, and more.

Fennec Fox Diet

fat sand rats

desert locusts

jerboas

Fennec foxes get most of their water from eating plants.

Their many adaptations make living in the desert look easy!

Fennec Fox Stats

| Least Concern | Near Threatened | Vulnerable | Endangered | Critically Endangered | Extinct in the Wild | Extinct |

conservation status: least concern

life span: up to 10 years

Glossary

adapted—changed over a long period of time

biome—a large area with certain plants, animals, and weather

burrows—holes or tunnels some animals dig for homes

coats—the hair or fur covering some animals

dunes—hills of sand made by the wind

insects—small animals with six legs and hard outer bodies; an insect's body is divided into three parts.

nocturnal—active at night

omnivores—animals that eat both plants and animals

pounce—to suddenly jump on something to catch it

predators—animals that hunt other animals for food

prey—animals that are hunted by other animals for food

reflects—bounces light and heat back

rodents—small animals that gnaw on their food; mice, rats, and squirrels are all rodents.

To Learn More

AT THE LIBRARY
Murray, Laura K. *In the Deserts*. Mankato, Minn.: Creative Education, 2019.

Pope, Kristen. *Fennec Foxes*. Mankato, Minn.: Child's World, 2015.

Siemens, Jared. *I Am a Fennec Fox*. New York, N.Y.: AV2 by Weigl, 2017.

ON THE WEB
FACTSURFER

Factsurfer.com gives you a safe, fun way to find more information.

1. Go to www.factsurfer.com.

2. Enter "fennec foxes" into the search box.

3. Click the "Surf" button and select your book cover to see a list of related web sites

With factsurfer.com, finding more information is just a click away.

Index

adaptations, 7, 9, 20
Africa, 4
biome, 5
burrows, 15
climb, 12
coats, 9
color, 11
dig, 17
dunes, 5, 12
ears, 8, 9, 16
feet, 9, 12
food, 18, 19, 20
fur, 10
hide, 11

nocturnal, 14
omnivores, 19
paws, 17
pounce, 17
predators, 11, 15
prey, 17
range, 4, 5
rodents, 16, 19
sand, 5, 11, 12, 16
status, 21
water, 20

The images in this book are reproduced through the courtesy of: CraigRJD/ Getty Images, front cover; Patrick Poendl, pp. 2-3; hagit berkovich, pp. 4, 8; Jose B. Ruiz/ Alamy, pp. 6, 12, 20; EdeWolf/ Getty Images, p. 7; siripong panasonthi, p. 9 (inset); Madeleine Dammann, p. 9; Getty Images, p. 10; LOOK-foto293231/ SuperStock, p. 11; CraigRJD, p. 13; buddhawut, p. 14; Konrad Wotheo/ SuperStock, p. 15; Juniors173858/ SuperStock, p. 16; RosaFrei, p. 17; ArtMediaFactory, p. 18; Fabi Fischer, p. 19 (top left); Vladimir Wrangel, p. 19 (top right); Yerbolat Shadrakhov, p. 19 (bottom); Tier und Naturfotografie/ SuperStock, p. 21; Amar and Isabelle Guillen/ Alamy, p. 23.